Famous Animals

Jill McDougall

Contents

Animal Stars 2

Animal Heroes 10

Animals in the News 16

Famous Animals 22

ANIMAL STARS

This book is about Marley the dog.

Skippy was a TV star.

People can be stars, but so can animals!

Babe was a movie star.

This dolphin was in the movie *Flipper*.

Some animals act in movies and on television. Some animals have had books made about them!

BENJI

Benji was a star. He acted in movies, such as *Benji*, and he was in lots of television shows. He was from a **dog shelter**, but then he found a good home.

Benji's real name was Higgins!

In his home, Benji learned lots of tricks. He could climb ladders. He could also yawn and sneeze.

Benji was so famous he even got letters from **fans**!

ALEX

Alex was a very smart parrot. He could say about 150 words. When he wanted something to eat, he said, "I want a nut!"

Alex could count up to six!

This lady is testing Alex.

Alex learned the names of seven colours and five shapes! People made books about Alex and made television shows about him.

Alex was famous for the things he learned to say and do.

BART

Bart was a huge brown bear. He was in lots of movies. People were amazed by Bart's acting.

Bart was trained to do 45 tricks.

Bart was a very smart bear. He learned to lie down, swim and stand up when he was told to.

Bart with his trainer Doug.

ANIMAL HEROES

This whale saved a diver.

This gorilla saved a boy who fell into her pen at a zoo.

Animals can be real life heroes.

This dog saved people trapped in a building.

This donkey saved soldiers in World War I.

Animals can be very brave. They can help people and other animals who are hurt or in danger.

SCARLETT

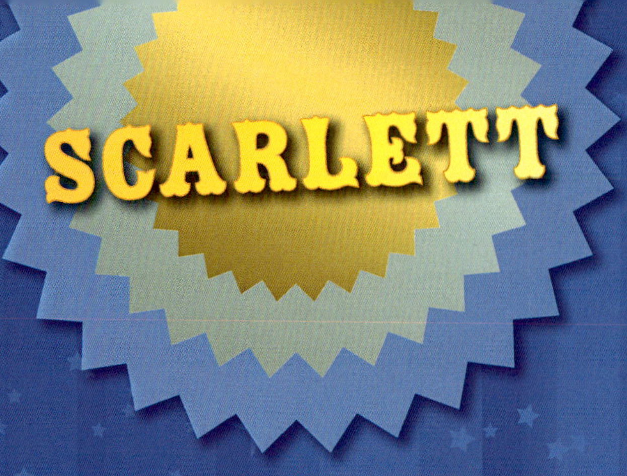

Scarlett was a **stray** cat with five kittens. One day, the place she lived in was on fire. Scarlett was burned but she picked up one kitten and took it out of the building.

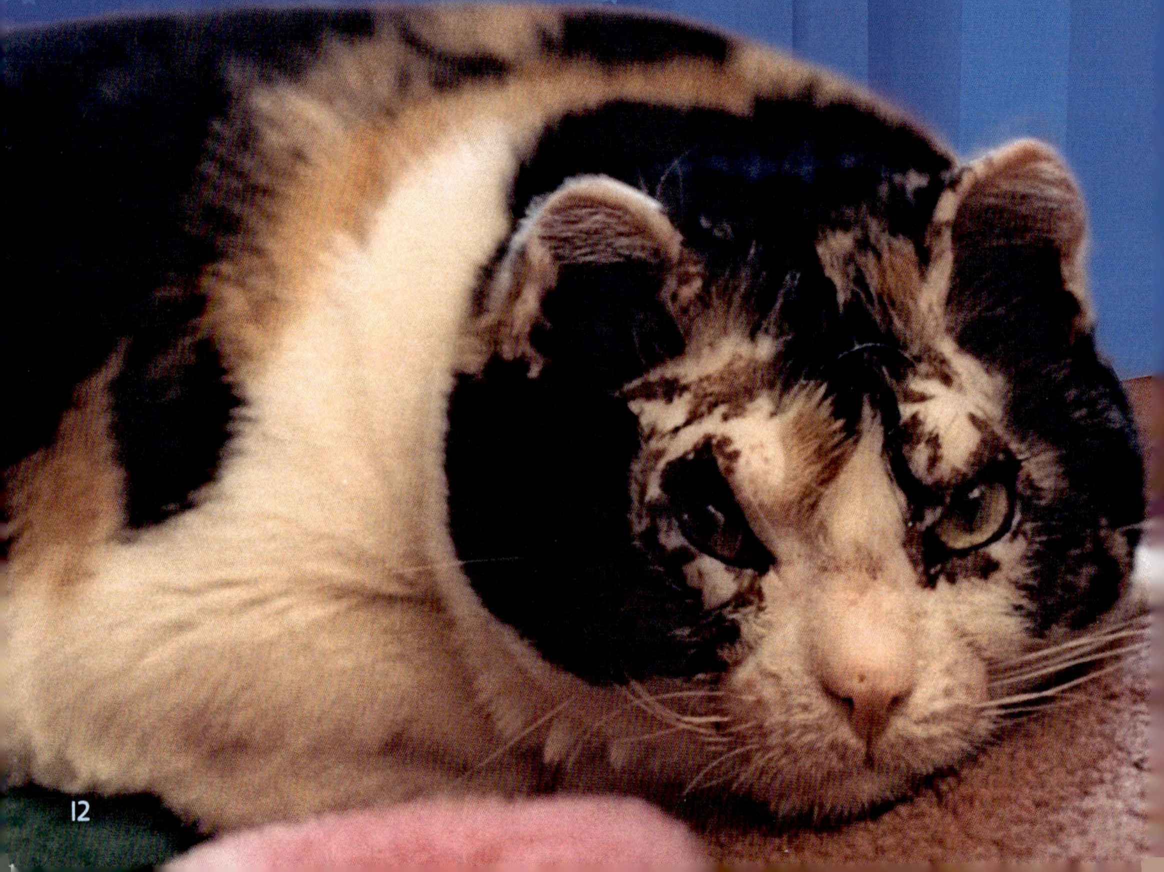

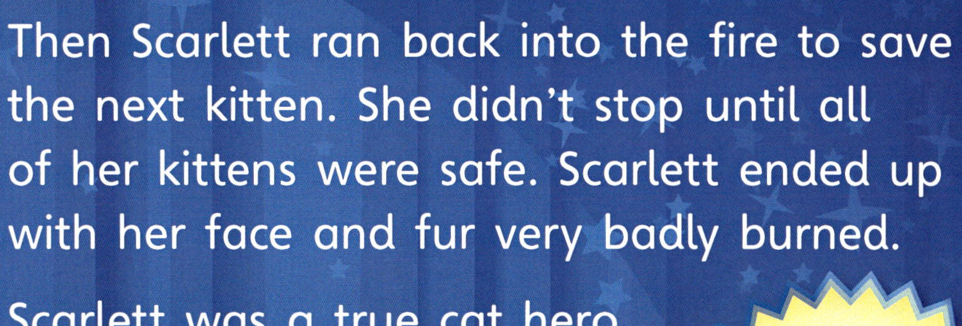

Then Scarlett ran back into the fire to save the next kitten. She didn't stop until all of her kittens were safe. Scarlett ended up with her face and fur very badly burned.

Scarlett was a true cat hero.

After the fire, lots of people wanted to **adopt** Scarlett! She went to a good home.

LULU

Lulu was a pet kangaroo that lived on a farm with Len and his family. One day a tree fell on Len and he was badly hurt. Lulu stayed with Len and made loud barking noises.

Lulu was given a **medal** for saving Len.

Lulu barked and barked until Len's family came over. They found Lulu with Len. They quickly took Len to hospital.

Clever Lulu had saved Len's life!

ANIMALS IN THE NEWS

Phar Lap is a famous race horse.

This baby elephant was saved from a hole.

Sometimes animals and their stories are in the news.

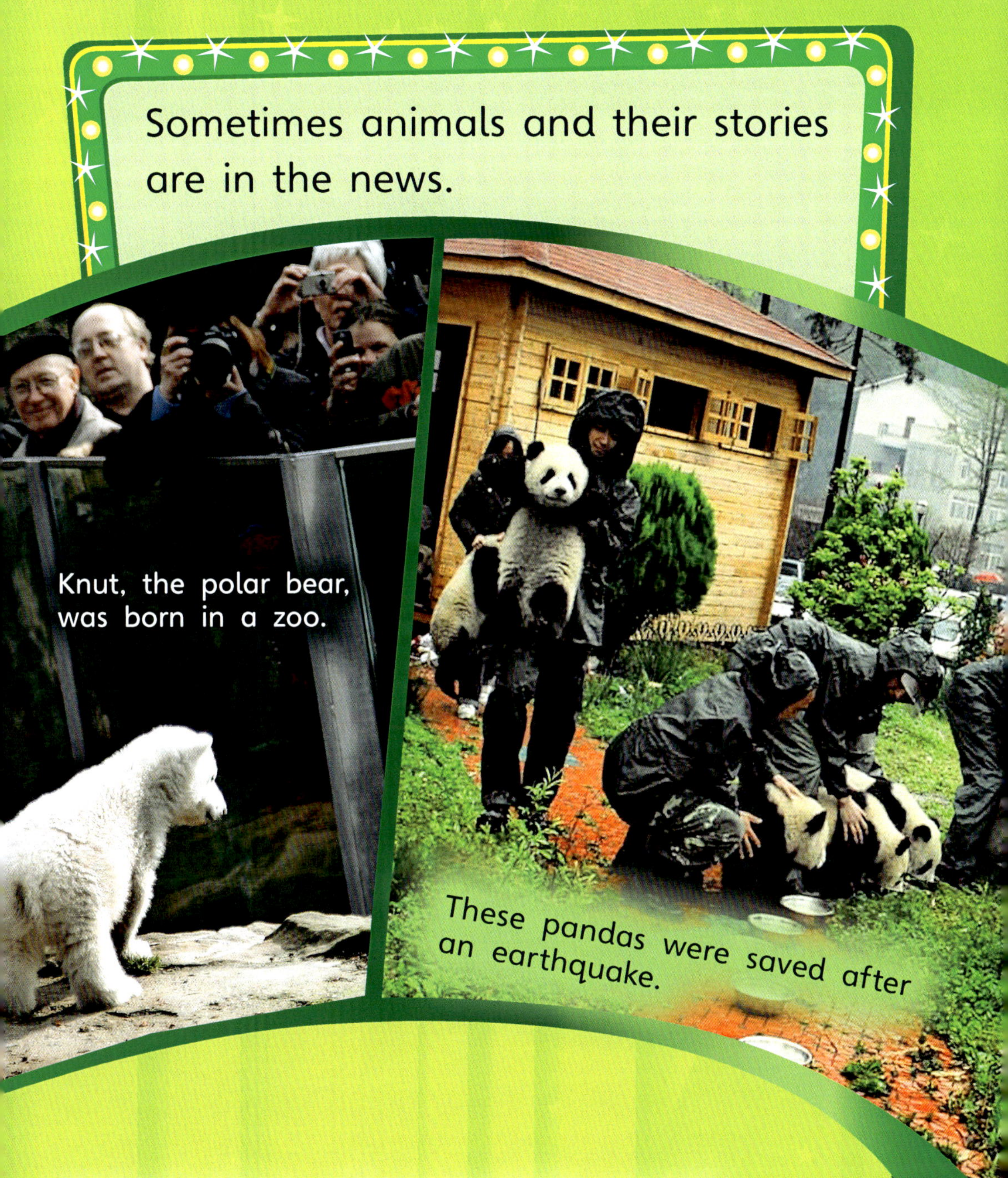

Knut, the polar bear, was born in a zoo.

These pandas were saved after an earthquake.

Animals from all around the world have been in the news.

SAM

Sam the koala was caught in a bushfire. Her paws got burned and she was very tired. A fire fighter found Sam and gave her a drink.

After the fire, Sam was looked after by a vet. The picture of Sam with the fire fighter was seen all over the world.

Sadly, Sam died a few months after the bushfire.

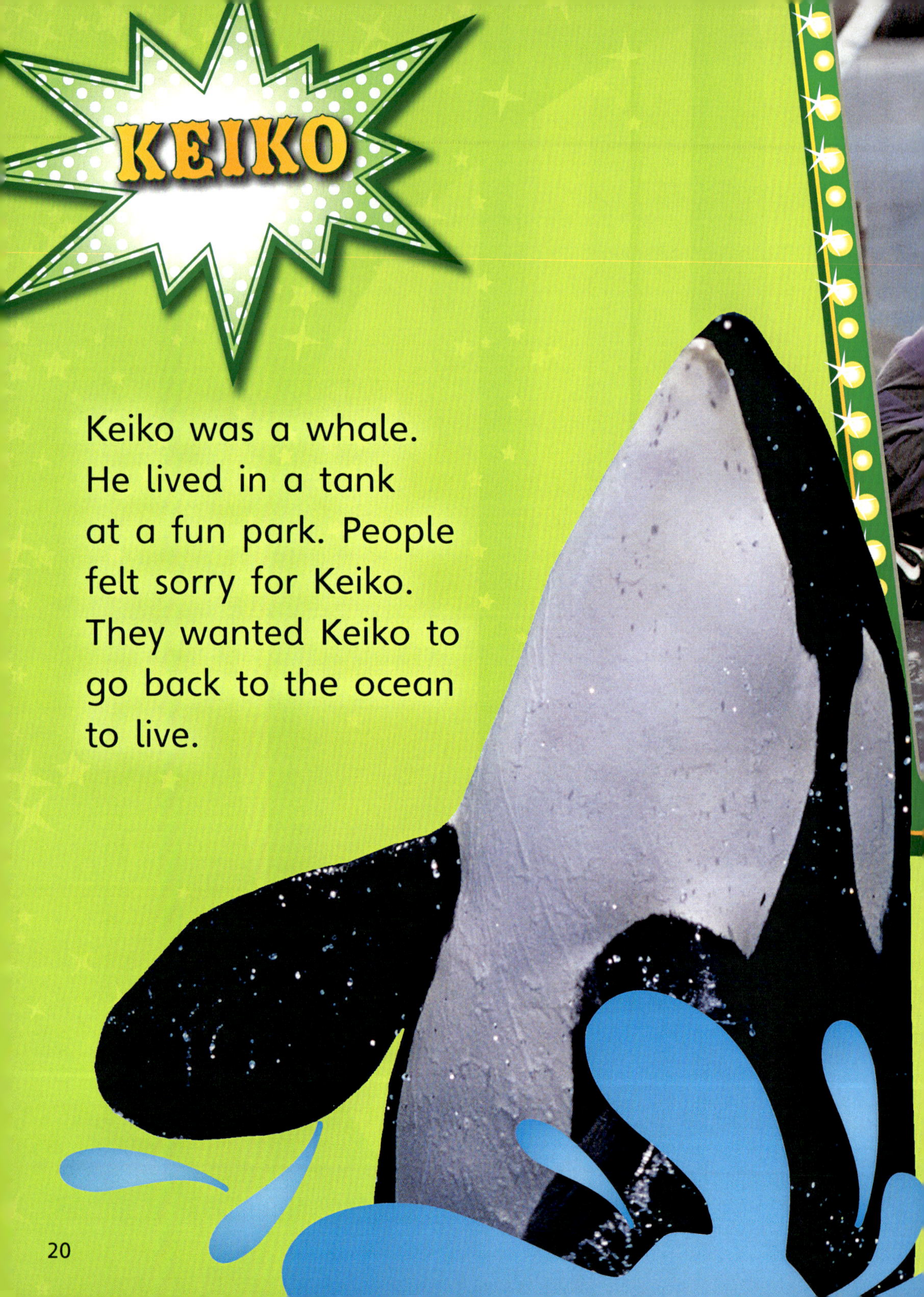

KEIKO

Keiko was a whale. He lived in a tank at a fun park. People felt sorry for Keiko. They wanted Keiko to go back to the ocean to live.

Keiko starred in a movie called *Free Willy*.

Lots of people wanted Keiko to be free. One day he was taken back to the ocean. He learned how to live with other whales in the wild.

Animals can be actors. They can be very brave. They can be famous!

Do you have a favourite famous animal?

Bart
Sam
Scarlett
Lulu
Keiko

Glossary

adopt	make a home for
dog shelter	a place where homeless dogs are kept
fans	people who like famous people or animals
medal	an award
stray	a homeless animal

Index

bear 8–9

cat 12–13

dog 4–5

kangaroo 14–15

koala 18–19

parrot 6–7

whale 20–21